Consumer Behavior

A COMPREHENSIVE HANDBOOK

Mr. Gaurav G. Gajbe
Dr. Siddhartha D. Nagdive
Mr. Manoj S. Jagnade

About the Book

The book comprehensively explores consumer behaviour, starting with the Introduction to Consumer Behaviour where it defines the concept, nature, and scope, and discusses its application in marketing. It delves into the Consumer Research Process and various factors influencing behaviour, including external influences like culture and social class, and internal influences such as needs and motivations, perception, and personality. The second unit, Consumer Motivation & Marketing Communications, examines the motivations behind consumer actions, drawing on theories like Maslow's Hierarchy of Needs and Freud's Theory of Motivation, and outlines the marketing communication process, highlighting interpersonal and persuasive communication systems.

Promotional Strategy is the focus of the third unit, detailing different strategies including pull and push promotions, retail and ecommerce strategies, and their importance and benefits. The fourth unit, Consumer Durables, provides insights into the Indian market, classifications like white and brown goods, and distinctions between durable and non-durable goods. Finally, the book addresses Consumer Personality, covering the role of personality in marketing, the concept of buyer persona, and various personality traits that affect consumer behaviour, such as extroversion, agreeableness and conscientiousness.

About the Authors

Mr. Gaurav G. Gajbe is a dedicated academic professional with a strong background in commerce and management. He holds an M.B.A. (2015), M. Com (2018), and an M.A. in Economics (2022), and is currently pursuing a Ph.D. in Commerce from Vidyabharti College, Seloo Wardha. Having cleared the MH-SET in Commerce in December 2020.

Gaurav aims to utilize his skills in a dynamic and competitive environment, contributing to the organization's growth and vision. He has three years of teaching experience at Umang Geetai College of Women's Education in Nagpur, handling subjects like Advanced Quantitative Techniques, Economics, and Business Law.

An optimistic, flexible, and disciplined individual, Gaurav has actively participated in volleyball during his undergraduate years and secured 9th merit in MBA at RTM Nagpur University in 2015. Proficient in English, Marathi, and Hindi, he enjoys playing volleyball in his leisure time. He is committed to fostering academic excellence and contributing positively to the educational landscape.

Dr. Siddhartha Nagdive, an Assistant Professor of Commerce at Vidyabharti College, brings wealth of knowledge to the book "Personal Selling and Service Marketing." With a robust academic background comprising M.COM., M.Phil., MIRPM, and Ph.D. in Commerce.

He has a proven track record in research and teaching. Residing in Wardha, Maharashtra, Dr. Nagdive can be reached at siddharth.sir191919@gmail.com . His extensive experience and dedication to the field make him a valuable contributor to this publication, offering deep insights into 'Consumer Behaviour' concepts.

Mr. Manoj Jagnade is an accomplished academic and professional with a diverse background in management, human resources, economics, and engineering. Currently pursuing a PhD in Management at Vidyabharti College, Seloo Wardha, RTM Nagpur University (2022-2025). He has extensive educational background and professional experience, combined with his commitment to continuous learning and skill development, make him a distinguished figure in the fields of management.

SYLLABUS

Unit I: Introduction to Consumer Behaviour & Factors affecting Consumer Behaviour

Definition, Nature, Scope, Consumer Behaviour's Applications in Marketing, Consumer research process, Factors influencing Consumer Behaviour– External Influences – Culture, Subculture, Social Class, Reference Groups, Family, Internal Influences– Needs & Motivations, Perception, Personality, Lifestyle, Values, Learning, Memory, Beliefs & Attitudes.

Unit II: Consumer Motivation & Marketing Communications

Consumer Motivation– Needs, Goals, Motive arousal, Maslow's Hierarchy of Needs, Freud's Theory of Motivation, Consumer Personality – Self-concept theory, Marketing Communication Process, Types of Communication systems – Interpersonal, Impersonal, Persuasive Communication

Unit III: Promotional Strategy

Definition, Types of Promotional Strategy, Pull Promotion Strategy, Push Promotion Strategy. Push Promotion Sales Promotion Strategy, Retail Promotion Strategy, Ecommerce Promotion Strategy, Importance of Promotional Strategy, Benefits of Promotional Strategies.

Unit IV: Consumer Durables

Information Consumer Durable Market within India, Classification of Consumer Durables, White Goods, Brown Goods, Shiney Goods, Imports and Exports in Consumer Durable Markets, Durable Goods Vs. Nondurable Goods, Durable Goods Companies, Credit Facility link with Consumer Durable, Consumer Durable Companies

Unit V: Consumer Personality

Definition, Personality Science in Marketing, Buyer Personas Optimize customer journey brand personality Extroversion and impulsive buying Agreeableness and word-of-mouth influence Conscientiousness and brand loyalty, interrelated Behaviour, Cognitive Patterns. Classification of Consumer Personality.

Reference Books:
1. Hawkins, Best and Coney, Consumer Behaviour, Tata McGraw Hill, New Delhi
2. John A Howard, Consumer Behaviour in Marketing Strategy, Prentice Hall New Delhi
3. Schiffman L G and Kanuk L Consumer Behaviour, Prentice Hall New Delhi
4. Anita Ghatak, Consumer Behaviour in India, D K Agencies (P) Ltd New Delhi
5. Sarkar A Problems of Consumer Behaviour in India, Discovery Publishing House New Delhi

List of Topics

Unit I: Introduction to Consumer Behaviour & Factors Affecting Consumer Behaviour

1. Definition
2. Nature
3. Scope
4. Consumer Behaviour's Applications in Marketing
5. Consumer Research Process
6. Factors Influencing Consumer Behaviour
   - External Influences
     - Culture
     - Subculture
     - Social Class
     - Reference Groups
     - Family
   - Internal Influences
     - Needs & Motivations
     - Perception
     - Personality
     - Lifestyle
     - Values
     - Learning
     - Memory
     - Beliefs & Attitudes

Unit II: Consumer Motivation & Marketing Communications

1. Consumer Motivation
   - Needs
   - Goals

- Motive Arousal
- Maslow's Hierarchy of Needs
- Freud's Theory of Motivation
2. Consumer Personality
    - Self-Concept Theory
3. Marketing Communication Process
4. Types of Communication Systems
    - Interpersonal Communication
    - Impersonal Communication
    - Persuasive Communication

Unit III: Promotional Strategy

1. Definition
2. Types of Promotional Strategy
3. Pull Promotion Strategy
4. Push Promotion Strategy
    - Push Promotion Sales Promotion Strategy
5. Retail Promotion Strategy
6. Ecommerce Promotion Strategy
7. Importance of Promotional Strategy
8. Benefits of Promotional Strategies

Unit IV: Consumer Durables

1. Information Consumer Durable Market within India
2. Classification of Consumer Durables
    - White Goods
    - Brown Goods
    - Shiny Goods
3. Imports and Exports in Consumer Durable Markets

4. Durable Goods Vs. Nondurable Goods
5. Durable Goods Companies
6. Credit Facility Link with Consumer Durable
7. Consumer Durable Companies

Unit V: Consumer Personality

1. Definition
2. Personality Science in Marketing
3. Buyer Personas
4. Optimize Customer Journey
5. Brand Personality
6. Extroversion and Impulsive Buying
7. Agreeableness and Word-of-Mouth Influence
8. Conscientiousness and Brand Loyalty
9. Interrelated Behaviour
10. Cognitive Patterns
11. Classification of Consumer Personality

Table of Contents

Sr. No.	Topic	Page No.
Unit I	Introduction to Consumer Behaviour & Factors Affecting Consumer Behaviour	08-16
Unit II	Consumer Motivation & Marketing Communications	17-24
Unit III	Promotional Strategy	25-35
Unit IV	Consumer Durables	36-44
Unit V	Consumer Personality	45-60

Unit I: Introduction to Consumer Behaviour & Factors affecting Consumer Behaviour

Definition of Consumer Behaviour

Consumer behaviour refers to the study of how individuals, groups, or organizations select, purchase, use, and dispose of goods, services, ideas, or experiences to satisfy their needs and desires. It encompasses the decision-making processes and actions involved in buying, using, and discarding products and services.

Nature of Consumer Behaviour

1. **Complexity**: Consumer behaviour is complex and influenced by various factors such as cultural, social, personal, and psychological aspects. These factors interact to shape how consumers make purchasing decisions.
2. **Dynamism**: Consumer behaviour is dynamic and constantly evolving. Changes in technology, lifestyle, and economic conditions can significantly impact how consumers behave in the marketplace.
3. **Individual Differences**: No two consumers are exactly alike. Personal preferences, lifestyles, and socio-economic backgrounds lead to diverse consumer behaviours.
4. **Decision-Making Process**: Consumer behaviour involves a decision-making process that includes problem recognition, information search, evaluation of alternatives, purchase decision, and post-purchase behaviour.

Scope of Consumer Behaviour

The scope of consumer behaviour is vast and encompasses several areas:

1. **Marketing Strategy**: Understanding consumer behaviour helps marketers design effective marketing strategies. By comprehending what drives consumer decisions, marketers can tailor their products, promotions, pricing, and distribution to meet consumer needs.
2. **Product Development**: Insights into consumer behaviour guide product development and innovation. Companies can create products that align with consumer preferences and fill gaps in the market.
3. **Customer Satisfaction and Retention**: Analysing consumer behaviour aids in enhancing customer satisfaction and retention. By understanding consumer expectations and experiences, businesses can improve their offerings and build long-term relationships with customers.
4. **Market Segmentation**: Consumer behaviour analysis facilitates market segmentation by identifying distinct groups of consumers with similar characteristics and needs. This allows for targeted marketing efforts.

5. **Predicting Trends**: Studying consumer behaviour helps predict market trends and shift Businesses can anticipate changes in consumer preferences and adapt accordingly.

Consumer Behaviour's Applications in Marketing

1. **Product Positioning**: Understanding how consumers perceive and evaluate products help marketers position their products effectively in the market. By emphasizing unique feature and benefits that resonate with target consumers, companies can differentiate their offering

2. **Advertising and Promotion**: Consumer behaviour insights guide advertising an promotional strategies. Marketers can craft messages that appeal to the motivations an emotions of their target audience. For example, luxury brands may focus on aspiration messaging, while convenience products may highlight ease of use.

3. **Pricing Strategies**: Knowledge of consumer behaviour aids in setting pricing strategie Understanding how consumers perceive value and price sensitivity helps in determinir optimal pricing points. For instance, premium pricing can be used for high-end products, whil penetration pricing can attract price-sensitive customers.

4. **Distribution Channels**: Analysing consumer behaviour informs decisions about distributio channels. Businesses can choose channels that align with consumer shopping preference whether it's online, in-store, or through direct sales.

5. **Customer Relationship Management (CRM)**: Consumer behaviour insights support CRM efforts by identifying key touchpoints and interactions that influence customer loyalt Personalization and targeted communication based on consumer preferences enhanc customer relationships.

6. **Brand Loyalty and Advocacy**: Understanding the factors that drive brand loyalty an advocacy helps marketers foster strong brand connections. By delivering consistent value an engaging with consumers meaningfully, brands can build loyal customer bases.

7. **Digital Marketing**: The digital landscape has transformed consumer behaviour, making essential for marketers to understand online consumer activities. Insights into how consumer navigate websites, social media, and online reviews guide digital marketing strategies.

8. **Ethical Marketing**: Consumer behaviour studies can also inform ethical marketing practice By understanding consumer concerns about sustainability, transparency, and corporate soci responsibility, businesses can adopt practices that align with consumer values.

Consumer Research Process

The consumer research process is a systematic approach to gathering, analysing, and interpreting information about consumers to understand their behaviour and preferences. This process helps businesses make informed decisions and develop effective marketing strategies.

Here are the key steps involved in the consumer research process:

1. **Problem Definition**
    - Clearly define the research problem or objective.
    - Identify the specific information needed to address the problem.
    - Formulate research questions or hypotheses.

2. **Research Design**
    - Choose the research method (qualitative, quantitative, or a combination).
    - Select the research approach (exploratory, descriptive, or causal).
    - Develop a detailed plan outlining the data collection methods, sample design, and data analysis techniques.

3. **Data Collection**
    - Collect primary data through surveys, interviews, focus groups, observations, or experiments.
    - Gather secondary data from existing sources such as reports, academic journals, industry publications, and online databases.
    - Ensure data collection methods are reliable and valid to obtain accurate information.

4. **Sampling**
    - Define the target population for the research.
    - Choose an appropriate sampling method (random, stratified, cluster, or convenience sampling).
    - Determine the sample size to ensure representativeness and statistical significance.

5. **Data Analysis**
    - Organize and process the collected data.
    - Use statistical tools and software to analyse quantitative data.
    - Interpret qualitative data through thematic analysis, content analysis, or narrative analysis.
    - Identify patterns, trends, and insights from the data.

6. **Interpretation and Findings**
    - Draw conclusions based on the analysed data.
    - Compare findings with the research questions or hypotheses.
    - Identify key insights and implications for business decisions.

7. **Report Preparation**
    - Compile the research findings into a comprehensive report.
    - Include an introduction, methodology, results, discussion, and recommendations.
    - Use visual aids such as charts, graphs, and tables to present data clearly.

8. **Decision Making**
    - Use the research findings to inform business decisions and marketing strategies.
    - Develop action plans based on the insights gained from the research.
    - Monitor and evaluate the outcomes of the implemented strategies.

9. **Follow-Up**
    - Review the effectiveness of the research process.
    - Identify any gaps or limitations in the research.
    - Plan future research to address new or ongoing questions.

Importance of Consumer Research

- **Informed Decision-Making**: Consumer research provides data-driven insights that help businesses make informed decisions about product development, marketing strategies, and customer engagement.
- **Understanding Consumer Needs**: By understanding consumer preferences and behaviours, businesses can tailor their offerings to meet customer needs effectively.
- **Competitive Advantage**: Research helps businesses stay ahead of competitors by identifying market trends and emerging opportunities.
- **Risk Mitigation**: Conducting thorough research reduces the risk of launching unsuccessful products or campaigns.
- **Customer Satisfaction**: Understanding consumer expectations allows businesses to improve customer satisfaction and build long-term loyalty.

The consumer research process is essential for businesses to gain a deep understanding of their target audience, make strategic decisions, and ultimately achieve business success.

Factors influencing Consumer Behaviour

Consumer behaviour is influenced by a complex interplay of various factors. These factors can be broadly categorized into four main types: cultural, social, personal, and psychological.

Cultural Factors

- **Culture**: The shared values, beliefs, and norms of a society that influence consumer preferences and behaviours.
- **Subculture**: Subgroups within a culture that have distinct values and lifestyles, such as ethnic groups, religious groups, and geographic regions.
- **Social Class**: The hierarchical division in a society, often based on income, education, occupation, and wealth, affecting consumer behaviour and purchasing patterns.

Social Factors

- **Reference Groups**: Groups that individuals look to for guidance on behaviours and attitudes. These can include family, friends, colleagues, and influential people.
- **Family**: The immediate family significantly influences consumer decisions, particularly through roles and responsibilities within the household.
- **Roles and Status**: An individual's position within groups (such as family, work, or social clubs) and the associated roles and status can affect their buying behaviour.

Personal Factors

- **Age and Life Cycle Stage**: Different age groups and life stages (e.g., single, married, with children) have distinct consumption patterns and preferences.
- **Occupation**: An individual's job influences their buying behaviour, with different professions having unique demands and preferences.
- **Economic Situation**: An individual's financial status, including income, savings, and credit availability, directly impacts their purchasing decisions.
- **Lifestyle**: The way a person lives their life, including activities, interests, and opinions, shapes their buying preferences and habits.
- **Personality and Self-Concept**: An individual's personality traits and self-image influence the brands and products they choose to buy.

Psychological Factors

- **Motivation**: The driving force behind consumer behaviour, which can be based on needs and desires. Maslow's hierarchy of needs is often used to understand consumer motivation.
- **Perception**: The process by which individuals select, organize, and interpret information to form a meaningful picture of the world. Perception affects how consumers see and respond to marketing messages.

- **Learning**: Changes in behaviour resulting from experience. Consumers learn from past experiences, and this influences their future purchase decisions.
- **Beliefs and Attitudes**: Beliefs are the assumptions that consumers hold about products services, while attitudes are their overall evaluations. Both beliefs and attitudes can significan influence buying behaviour.

Understanding these factors helps businesses develop targeted marketing strategies that resonate w their audience, improve product offerings, and enhance customer satisfaction.

External Influences of Consumer Behaviour

Consumer behaviour is significantly shaped by various external influences that impact their decisio making processes. These influences include culture, subculture, social class, reference groups, a family.

Culture

Culture is the broadest and most pervasive influence on consumer behaviour. It encompasses t values, beliefs, customs, and norms shared by a group of people, which guide their behaviour a preferences. Cultural factors influence what products consumers buy, how they use them, and ho they dispose of them. For example, cultural differences can affect dietary habits, fashion choices, a holiday celebrations. Marketers must understand cultural nuances to effectively target differe consumer groups and tailor their marketing strategies accordingly.

Subculture

Within a larger culture, there are **subcultures** that have distinct values and lifestyles. Subcultures c be based on factors such as ethnicity, religion, geographic region, and age. These subgroups exhib specific purchasing behaviours that differ from the broader culture. For instance, the buying patter of teenagers can differ significantly from those of older adults, and ethnic subcultures may have uniq preferences for food, clothing, and entertainment. By recognizing and addressing the needs different subcultures, marketers can create more targeted and effective marketing campaigns.

Social Class

Social class is a hierarchical division in society based on factors such as income, educatio occupation, and wealth. It influences consumer behaviour by affecting preferences, purchasing pow and access to resources. Higher social classes may prioritize luxury and status-oriented products, wh lower social classes may focus on functionality and affordability. Social class also affects med consumption habits, brand loyalty, and the channels through which consumers shop. Marketers ne understand the social class dynamics of their target audience to position their products appropriately and select suitable marketing channels.

Reference Groups

Reference groups are groups that individuals look to for guidance on behaviours and attitudes. These can include family, friends, colleagues, or celebrities. Reference groups influence consumer decisions by providing information, reinforcing norms, and shaping perceptions. For example, a person might buy a particular brand of clothing because it is popular among their peer group or endorsed by a favourite celebrity. Marketers can leverage the influence of reference groups through strategies like influencer marketing, where products are promoted by individuals who have a significant impact on their followers' purchasing decisions.

Family

Family is one of the most important reference groups and has a profound impact on consumer behaviour. Family members influence the decision-making process, both as individuals and collectively. For example, parents may make purchasing decisions for their children, or a family's lifestyle and consumption patterns may be influenced by the collective preferences of its members. Understanding the role of family in consumer behaviour is crucial for marketers, especially in categories such as household goods, children's products, and family-oriented services. Marketers can tailor their messages to address the needs and preferences of different family members, ensuring their products appeal to the entire household.

Internal Influences of Consumer Behaviour

Consumer behaviour is profoundly influenced by various internal factors. These factors originate within the individual and shape how they perceive, evaluate, and act on purchasing decisions. Let's explore these internal influences in detail:

Needs & Motivations

Needs are fundamental human requirements that drive behaviour. They can be physiological (like hunger and thirst) or psychological (like the need for esteem and belonging). **Motivations** are the driving forces behind these needs, propelling individuals to take action to satisfy them. Maslow's Hierarchy of Needs is often used to understand this, categorizing needs from basic physiological requirements to self-actualization.

Perception

Perception is the process by which individuals select, organize, and interpret sensory information to make sense of their environment. It involves how consumers see, hear, and feel about a product or service. Perception can be influenced by various factors such as selective attention (noticing certain aspects of an advertisement), selective distortion (interpreting information in a way that fits preconceptions), and selective retention (remembering information that supports beliefs and forgetting what doesn't).

Personality

Personality refers to the unique psychological characteristics that consistently influence how a person responds to their environment. Traits such as extroversion, openness to experience, and conscientiousness can affect consumer choices. For example, an adventurous person may be more inclined to try new products and brands.

Lifestyle

Lifestyle reflects how individuals live, spend their time, and allocate their resources. It encompasses activities, interests, and opinions (AIO). A person's lifestyle influences their buying behaviour, such as preferences for leisure activities, clothing, and food. For instance, a health-conscious individual might prefer organic foods and fitness-related products.

Values

Values are deeply held beliefs about what is important in life. They guide behaviour and influence attitudes and decisions. Values can be shaped by culture, family, and personal experiences. Consumers often choose products that align with their values, such as eco-friendly products for those who value sustainability.

Learning

Learning involves changes in behaviour resulting from experience. It affects future behaviour based on past interactions with products and brands. Learning can occur through classical conditioning (associating a product with positive experiences), operant conditioning (rewarding behaviours to reinforce them), and observational learning (imitating behaviours seen in others).

Memory

Memory plays a crucial role in consumer behaviour by storing and retrieving information about past experiences. It influences decision-making and brand recall. Marketers aim to create positive and memorable experiences that consumers can recall when making purchasing decisions. Memory is impacted by how information is encoded, stored, and retrieved.

Beliefs & Attitudes

Beliefs are descriptive thoughts that a person holds about something, while **attitudes** are a person's consistently favourable or unfavourable evaluations, feelings, and tendencies towards an object or idea. These form over time through experiences and learning and strongly influence consumer behaviour. Positive attitudes towards a brand can lead to brand loyalty, while negative attitudes can deter purchases.

Unit II: Consumer Motivation & Marketing Communications

Consumer Motivation

Consumer motivation is a fundamental aspect of understanding consumer behaviour. It refers to t driving forces behind individuals' actions to fulfil their needs and achieve their goals. Motivation consumer behaviour is primarily influenced by needs, goals, and the process of motive arousal.

Needs

Needs are the essential requirements that motivate behaviour. They can be classified into seve categories:

1. **Physiological Needs**: These are the necessities for survival, such as food, water, shelter, a sleep. They are the most fundamental needs and must be satisfied before other needs can addressed.

2. **Safety Needs**: Once physiological needs are met, individuals seek safety and security. Th includes personal safety, financial security, health, and well-being.

3. **Social Needs**: Humans are inherently social beings, and they need to belong and be accept by others. Social needs encompass relationships, love, affection, and a sense of belonging.

4. **Esteem Needs**: Esteem needs involve the desire for respect, self-esteem, recognition, a achievement. Fulfilling these needs enhances an individual's confidence and sense of worth

5. **Self-Actualization Needs**: At the highest level of Maslow's hierarchy of needs, se actualization represents the pursuit of personal growth, self-fulfilment, and realizing one's f potential.

Goals

Goals are specific outcomes or achievements that individuals strive to attain. They provide directic and purpose to behaviour. Goals can be short-term or long-term and are influenced by an individua needs and motivations. Goals are essential for several reasons:

1. **Guidance**: Goals provide a clear direction for behaviour, helping individuals focus the efforts on achieving specific outcomes.

2. **Motivation**: Setting goals enhances motivation by creating a sense of purpose and urgency.

3. **Evaluation**: Goals serve as benchmarks for evaluating progress and success. They enab individuals to measure their achievements and adjust their strategies if needed.

4. **Satisfaction**: Achieving goals brings a sense of accomplishment and satisfaction, reinforcir positive behaviour and encouraging further goal setting.

Motive Arousal

Motive arousal is the process through which an individual's needs become active drivers of behaviour. This arousal can be triggered by various factors:

1. **Internal Stimuli**: These are physiological or psychological conditions within the individual that prompt a need. For example, hunger (a physiological need) arouses the motive to seek food.
2. **External Stimuli**: External factors such as advertising, social influences, and environmental cues can arouse motives. For instance, a billboard advertising a new smartphone can arouse the motive to purchase it.
3. **Emotional Arousal**: Emotions play a significant role in motive arousal. Positive emotions like happiness and excitement can motivate individuals to seek pleasurable experiences, while negative emotions like fear and anxiety can drive them to avoid threats.
4. **Cognitive Processes**: The way individuals perceive and interpret information can arouse motives. For example, learning about the health benefits of exercise can arouse the motive to engage in physical activity.

Maslow's Hierarchy of Needs

Maslow's Hierarchy of Needs is a motivational theory in psychology proposed by Abraham Maslow in 1943. It is often depicted as a pyramid with five levels of needs, arranged in a hierarchy. The basic premise of Maslow's theory is that individuals are motivated to fulfil their needs in a specific order, starting with the most fundamental physiological needs and moving towards self-actualization. Here is a detailed look at each level:

1. **Physiological Needs**: These are the most basic human needs for survival. They include necessities such as air, water, food, shelter, sleep, and clothing. Until these needs are met, an individual cannot focus on higher-level needs.
2. **Safety Needs**: Once physiological needs are satisfied, the focus shifts to safety and security. This includes personal security, financial security, health and well-being, and protection against accidents and illness.
3. **Social Needs**: Also known as love and belongingness needs, these include relationships, friendships, intimacy, and family. Humans are inherently social beings, and fulfilling these needs is crucial for emotional health and well-being.
4. **Esteem Needs**: Esteem needs are divided into two categories: (a) self-esteem, which includes self-respect, achievement, and independence; and (b) esteem from others, which includes recognition, status, and respect from peers. Fulfilment of these needs leads to feelings of confidence and accomplishment.

5. **Self-Actualization Needs**: This is the highest level in Maslow's hierarchy. Self-actualization refers to the realization of one's potential, self-fulfilment, seeking personal growth, and peak experiences. It involves becoming the most that one can be and achieving personal goals and aspirations.

Maslow later expanded the hierarchy to include cognitive and aesthetic needs (the desire for knowledge and appreciation of beauty) and self-transcendence (a focus beyond the self, toward altruism and spirituality).

Freud's Theory of Motivation

Sigmund Freud's Theory of Motivation is based on his psychoanalytic theory, which emphasizes the role of unconscious desires and instincts in shaping behaviour. Freud proposed that human behaviour is driven by three main components of the psyche: the id, ego, and superego. Here's a closer look at these components and their role in motivation:

1. **Id**: The id is the primitive and instinctual part of the psyche that operates based on the pleasure principle. It seeks immediate gratification of basic desires and drives, such as hunger, thirst and sexual impulses. The id is entirely unconscious and does not consider reality or social norms.

2. **Ego**: The ego develops to mediate between the unrealistic demands of the id and the external world. It operates based on the reality principle, considering what is practical and socially acceptable. The ego tries to satisfy the id's desires in a realistic and appropriate manner, balancing immediate gratification with long-term goals.

3. **Superego**: The superego represents internalized societal and parental standards of right and wrong. It operates based on the morality principle, striving for perfection and judging the ego's actions and thoughts. The superego aims to control the id's impulses and persuade the ego to pursue moralistic goals rather than simply realistic ones.

Freud believed that human behaviour and motivation are influenced by the dynamic interaction among these three components. He also emphasized the role of unconscious processes, suggesting that many of our motivations are hidden from our conscious awareness. Freud's theory highlights the importance of early childhood experiences, repressed desires, and unresolved conflicts in shaping individual's motivations and behaviours.

Consumer Personality – Self-Concept Theory

Understanding consumer personality is crucial for marketers aiming to predict and influence buying behaviours. One key theory in this field is the Self-Concept Theory, which delves into how individuals perceive themselves and how these perceptions shape their consumption choices. The Self-Concept Theory posits that individuals have multiple self-concepts, including the actual self, ideal self, and social self, each playing a distinct role in consumer behaviour.

The Actual Self

The **actual self** refers to an individual's perception of who they currently are. This encompasses all the attributes and characteristics that a person believes they possess, including their strengths, weaknesses, and unique traits. The actual self-influences consumer behaviour in a way that individuals seek products and services that align with their true self-image. For instance, a person who sees themselves as health-conscious is likely to purchase organic foods and fitness-related products.

The Ideal Self

The **ideal self** represents the person an individual aspires to become. It includes dreams, ambitions, and the qualities they wish to embody. The ideal self is often shaped by personal goals, role models, and societal expectations. Consumers are motivated to purchase products and services that they believe will help them bridge the gap between their actual and ideal selves. For example, someone who aspires to be more sophisticated may invest in high-end fashion or luxury vehicles to project their desired image.

The Social Self

The **social self** pertains to how individuals perceive themselves in a social context, including how they think others see them. It encompasses social roles, relationships, and the desire for social acceptance and belonging. This aspect of self-concept drives consumers to make purchases that enhance their social standing or help them fit into desired social groups. For instance, teenagers might buy the latest smartphone model to feel accepted by their peers.

Implications of Self-Concept Theory in Marketing

Understanding the different dimensions of self-concept helps marketers craft strategies that resonate with consumers on a deeper level. Here are some key implications:

1. **Targeted Marketing**: By recognizing the self-concepts that different consumer segments prioritize, marketers can create targeted campaigns that speak directly to these aspects. For example, fitness brands can appeal to the actual self of health-conscious individuals by emphasizing the authenticity of their health benefits.

2. **Brand Positioning**: Brands can position themselves as facilitators of the ideal self, promising transformation and improvement. Cosmetic companies often leverage this by promoting products that claim to enhance one's appearance, thereby aligning with the consumer's ideal self.

3. **Social Influence**: Marketers can leverage the social self by creating campaigns that highlight social proof and acceptance. For example, showcasing testimonials from satisfied customers or featuring influencers can appeal to the consumer's desire for social validation.

4. **Emotional Connection**: Brands that understand and align with a consumer's self-concept can create a strong emotional bond. This connection can lead to increased brand loyalty and advocacy, as consumers feel that the brand truly understands and represents them.

5. **Customization and Personalization**: Offering personalized products and experiences can cater to the unique self-concepts of individual consumers. For example, customizable fashion items or bespoke services allow consumers to express their actual or ideal selves more precisely.

Marketing Communication Process

The marketing communication process is a series of steps that organizations use to convey their messages effectively to their target audience. This process ensures that the message is not only delivered but also received and understood as intended. Here's a detailed look at the key components of the marketing communication process:

1. **Sender**
   - The **sender** is the organization or individual responsible for creating and delivering the message. This could be a company, marketing team, or brand. The sender initiates the communication process by formulating the message.

2. **Encoding**
   - **Encoding** involves transforming the sender's ideas into a format that can be transmitted to the audience. This includes selecting appropriate words, symbols, images, and sounds that will effectively communicate the intended message. The encoding process must consider the preferences, understanding, and cultural background of the target audience.

3. **Message**
   - The **message** is the content of the communication. It includes the information, emotions, and values that the sender wants to convey. The message can be conveyed through various forms such as advertisements, social media posts, emails, press releases, or any other marketing material.

4. **Medium**
   - The **medium** is the channel through which the message is transmitted. This could be traditional media (television, radio, print), digital media (websites, social media, email), or in-person methods (events, face-to-face interactions). The choice of medium depends on the target audience and the nature of the message.

5. **Receiver**

- The **receiver** is the individual or group for whom the message is intended. The receiver decodes the message based on their own perceptions, attitudes, and experiences. Understanding the receiver's profile is crucial for effective communication.

6. **Decoding**
   - **Decoding** is the process by which the receiver interprets and makes sense of the encoded message. The effectiveness of decoding depends on the clarity of the message and the receiver's ability to understand it. Misinterpretations can occur if the message is not clear or if there is a disconnect between the sender's and receiver's perspectives.

7. **Feedback**
   - **Feedback** is the response from the receiver back to the sender. It indicates whether the message has been understood as intended. Feedback can be direct (such as responses to surveys or comments) or indirect (such as changes in purchasing behaviour or social media engagement). Feedback helps the sender refine and improve future communications.

8. **Noise**
   - **Noise** refers to any external or internal interference that can distort or hinder the communication process. This includes physical noise (background sounds), psychological noise (prejudices, preconceptions), and semantic noise (misunderstanding of words or symbols). Minimizing noise is essential for clear communication.

Importance of the Marketing Communication Process

- **Clarity and Consistency**: A well-defined process ensures that the message is clear, consistent, and aligned with the brand's values and objectives.
- **Target Audience Engagement**: By understanding and addressing the needs and preferences of the target audience, marketers can create messages that resonate and engage effectively.
- **Brand Awareness and Perception**: Consistent and effective communication helps in building and maintaining brand awareness and a positive brand perception among the audience.
- **Customer Relationships**: Effective communication fosters strong relationships with customers by ensuring that their needs are understood and addressed.
- **Feedback and Improvement**: The feedback mechanism allows marketers to assess the effectiveness of their communications and make necessary adjustments.

Types of Communication Systems

Effective communication is pivotal in conveying messages and facilitating understanding among individuals or groups. In the realm of marketing and business, three primary types of communication systems are Interpersonal, Impersonal, and Persuasive Communication. Each serves distinct purposes and employs different techniques to achieve its goals.

Interpersonal Communication

Interpersonal communication involves direct, face-to-face interaction between two or more individuals. This type of communication is characterized by personal contact and the exchange of information, ideas, and feelings. Interpersonal communication can be verbal (spoken words) or non-verbal (body language, facial expressions, gestures). Key attributes include:

- **Two-Way Exchange**: Interpersonal communication is a two-way process, allowing immediate feedback and adjustments to the message.
- **Personalized**: Messages are tailored to the individual or small group, making the communication more relevant and engaging.
- **Contextual**: The context of the interaction, such as the setting and relationship between the communicators, significantly influences the communication process.
- **Emotional Connection**: This type of communication often involves an emotional component, helping to build relationships and trust.

Interpersonal communication is essential in various settings, such as negotiations, customer service, and team collaborations. It allows for a deeper understanding and fosters strong connections.

Impersonal Communication

Impersonal communication refers to the exchange of information that is not directed at a specific individual and does not involve personal contact. This type of communication is often used for mass communication, where the message is intended for a broad audience. Attributes of impersonal communication include:

- **One-Way Communication**: Typically, impersonal communication is a one-way process where feedback is not immediate or direct.
- **Generalized Messages**: The messages are designed to be broad and applicable to a large audience, lacking personalization.
- **Mass Media Channels**: Common channels include television, radio, newspapers, and digital platforms such as websites and social media.
- **Informative or Directive**: Impersonal communication often aims to inform, educate, or direct the audience on specific issues or actions.

...personal communication is effective for reaching a wide audience and disseminating information quickly. However, it may lack the emotional connection and immediate feedback that interpersonal communication provides.

Persuasive Communication

Persuasive communication aims to influence the attitudes, beliefs, or behaviours of the audience. It can be both interpersonal and impersonal, depending on the context and medium used. Key aspects of persuasive communication include:

- **Goal-Oriented**: The primary objective is to persuade the audience to adopt a certain viewpoint, take an action, or change their behaviour.
- **Emotional Appeal**: Persuasive communication often employs emotional appeals to connect with the audience and evoke a response.
- **Logical Arguments**: It uses logical reasoning and evidence to support the message, making it more convincing.
- **Credibility**: The credibility of the communicator is crucial in persuasive communication. Trustworthy and authoritative sources are more likely to influence the audience.

Persuasive communication is widely used in advertising, marketing campaigns, public relations, and political speeches. It involves various techniques, such as storytelling, testimonials, and rhetorical questions, to engage and convince the audience.

Unit III: Promotional Strategy

Definition of Promotional Strategy

A **promotional strategy** is a comprehensive plan designed by businesses to create awareness a persuade consumers about their products or services, ultimately influencing their purchase decisio It encompasses various marketing tools and techniques aimed at reaching the target audien conveying the intended message, and achieving the desired marketing objectives.

Types of Promotional Strategy

Promotional strategies can be categorized into several types, each utilizing different channels a techniques to achieve specific goals. Here are some common types:

1. Advertising

Advertising involves paying for space or time to promote a product, service, or brand. It is typica a one-way communication aimed at a broad audience. Advertising can be conducted through vario media, including television, radio, print (newspapers and magazines), online platforms (social med websites), and outdoor advertising (billboards, transit ads). The key objective is to inform, persuad and remind consumers about the brand and its offerings.

2. Sales Promotion

Sales promotion includes short-term incentives to encourage the purchase or sale of a product service. These can be directed at both consumers and trade channels (retailers and distributor Examples of sales promotions are discounts, coupons, contests, free samples, and loyalty program The goal is to boost sales quickly and effectively.

3. Public Relations (PR)

Public relations involve managing the public image and reputation of a brand. It focuses on buildi positive relationships with the media, the public, and other stakeholders. PR activities include pre releases, media events, sponsorships, community involvement, and crisis management. The aim is generate favourable publicity and create a positive brand image.

4. Personal Selling

Personal selling is a direct form of promotion where sales representatives interact with potent customers to persuade them to make a purchase. This approach is highly personalized and involv building relationships with customers, understanding their needs, and providing tailored solutior

personal selling is common in industries such as real estate, pharmaceuticals, and high-end consumer goods.

Direct Marketing

Direct marketing targets specific individuals or groups with personalized messages. This can be achieved through direct mail, email marketing, telemarketing, and SMS marketing. Direct marketing allows for direct engagement with customers, making it easier to measure the effectiveness of the campaign and gather feedback.

Digital Marketing

Digital marketing utilizes online platforms and technologies to promote products and services. This includes search engine optimization (SEO), social media marketing, content marketing, pay-per-click (PPC) advertising, and influencer marketing. Digital marketing allows businesses to reach a global audience, track and analyse consumer behavior, and optimize campaigns in real-time.

Content Marketing

Content marketing focuses on creating and distributing valuable, relevant, and consistent content to attract and engage a target audience. The goal is to build a strong relationship with consumers by providing useful information, ultimately driving profitable customer action. Examples of content marketing include blogs, articles, videos, infographics, and podcasts.

Sponsorship and Events

Sponsorship and events involve supporting events, activities, or organizations financially or through services. This strategy aims to enhance brand visibility and association with positive experiences. Sponsorship can range from sports events to cultural festivals, while events can include trade shows, product launches, and webinars.

Pull Promotion Strategy

Pull promotion strategy is a marketing approach aimed at generating consumer demand for a product or service, which in turn encourages retailers and distributors to stock and sell it. The goal is to create a strong consumer interest and desire for the product, effectively "pulling" it through the distribution channels. Key components of pull strategy include:

1. **Advertising**: Extensive advertising campaigns to build brand awareness and consumer interest. This can include television commercials, online ads, social media marketing, and print advertisements.

2. **Content Marketing**: Providing valuable and engaging content to attract and educate potential customers. This could involve blog posts, videos, infographics, and social media content.

3. **Promotions and Discounts**: Offering promotional deals, discounts, and special offers to entice consumers to try the product.

4. **Public Relations**: Building a positive brand image through public relations activities, such as press releases, media coverage, and influencer partnerships.

5. **Social Media Engagement**: Actively engaging with consumers on social media platforms to create a community around the brand and encourage word-of-mouth marketing.

Example: A smartphone manufacturer launches a new model and uses a pull strategy by running a series of engaging advertisements, collaborating with tech influencers for reviews, and offering limited-time discounts to generate consumer interest and demand.

Push Promotion Strategy

Push promotion strategy is a marketing approach that focuses on pushing a product through the distribution channels to the end consumers. This strategy involves promoting the product to retailers, wholesalers, and distributors, encouraging them to stock and sell the product. Key components of push strategy include:

1. **Trade Shows and Exhibitions**: Participating in trade shows and exhibitions to showcase products to potential retailers and distributors.

2. **Sales Promotions**: Providing incentives to retailers and distributors, such as discounts, bonuses, or free samples, to encourage them to stock and promote the product.

3. **Personal Selling**: Using a sales force to directly communicate with retailers and distributors, persuading them to carry the product.

4. **Point-of-Sale Displays**: Creating attractive displays and merchandising materials to encourage retailers to prominently feature the product in their stores.

5. **Distribution Deals**: Negotiating favourable terms and conditions with retailers and distributors to ensure the product is readily available to consumers.

Example: A beverage company launches a new drink and employs a push strategy by offering promotional deals to retailers, setting up eye-catching point-of-sale displays in stores, and having sales representatives work directly with distributors to secure shelf space.

Push Promotion Sales Promotion Strategy

push promotion sales promotion strategy focuses on pushing products through the distribution channels to the end consumers. This approach aims to create demand by encouraging retailers, wholesalers, and distributors to stock and sell the product. The strategy involves various sales promotion techniques designed to incentivize channel partners and ensure that the product reaches the final consumer efficiently. Here are the key components of a push promotion sales promotion strategy:

Trade Shows and Exhibitions

- **Purpose**: To showcase products to potential retailers, wholesalers, and distributors.
- **Activities**: Participating in industry trade shows and exhibitions, setting up booths, and demonstrating products.
- **Benefits**: Increases product visibility, builds relationships with channel partners, and facilitates direct engagement with potential buyers.

Trade Promotions

- **Purpose**: To incentivize retailers and distributors to stock and promote the product.
- **Activities**: Offering trade promotions such as bulk discounts, rebates, and special pricing for large orders.
- **Benefits**: Encourages bulk purchases, enhances product availability, and motivates channel partners to prioritize the product.

Personal Selling

- **Purpose**: To engage directly with retailers, wholesalers, and distributors to persuade them to carry the product.
- **Activities**: Deploying a sales force to visit and interact with channel partners, conducting sales presentations, and addressing any concerns or objections.
- **Benefits**: Builds strong relationships, allows for personalized communication, and facilitates immediate feedback and negotiation.

Point-of-Sale (POS) Displays

- **Purpose**: To attract consumers' attention and encourage impulse purchases at retail locations.
- **Activities**: Designing and providing attractive POS displays, including signage, standees, and product showcases, to retailers.

- **Benefits**: Increases product visibility, enhances brand presence in stores, and encourages retailers to feature the product prominently.

5. Trade Incentives

- **Purpose**: To motivate channel partners to actively promote and sell the product.
- **Activities**: Offering incentives such as cash bonuses, free goods, or exclusive deals to retailers and distributors who achieve specific sales targets.
- **Benefits**: Drives sales performance, fosters healthy competition among channel partners, and incentivizes proactive promotion.

6. Cooperative Advertising

- **Purpose**: To support retailers and distributors in their local advertising efforts.
- **Activities**: Providing financial assistance or resources for advertising the product in local markets, including print ads, radio spots, and digital campaigns.
- **Benefits**: Enhances local market penetration, aligns branding efforts, and shares the cost of advertising with channel partners.

7. Training and Support

- **Purpose**: To equip channel partners with the knowledge and skills to effectively sell the product.
- **Activities**: Conducting training sessions, providing sales manuals, and offering ongoing support and resources.
- **Benefits**: Improves product knowledge, enhances sales techniques, and boosts confidence among channel partners.

Retail Promotion Strategy

A retail promotion strategy is designed to increase customer traffic, enhance shopping experience, and boost sales within a retail environment. This strategy employs various promotional tools and techniques to attract and retain customers. Here are key components of an effective retail promotion strategy:

In-Store Promotions

In-store promotions create excitement and encourage purchases by offering incentives directly in the retail location. This can include:

- **Discounts and Sales**: Temporary price reductions on specific items or store-wide sales to encourage immediate purchases.
- **Buy One, Get One (BOGO) Offers**: Promotions where customers receive a free or discounted item when they purchase another at full price.
- **Product Bundling**: Offering a set of complementary products at a reduced price to increase the average transaction value.
- **Flash Sales**: Limited time offers that create urgency and drive quick sales.

Loyalty Programs

Loyalty programs reward repeat customers and encourage ongoing patronage. Key elements include:

- **Points Systems**: Customers earn points for purchases, which can be redeemed for discounts, free products, or other rewards.
- **Exclusive Offers**: Special deals and promotions for loyalty program members only.
- **Tiered Rewards**: Different levels of rewards based on the amount spent or frequency of visits, incentivizing higher spending and more frequent shopping.

Digital Marketing

Digital marketing promotes the retail store and its offerings through online channels. Key tactics include:

- **Social Media Marketing**: Engaging with customers on platforms like Facebook, Instagram, and Twitter, and running targeted ads to increase store visits.
- **Email Campaigns**: Sending newsletters, special offers, and personalized promotions to a subscriber list to drive traffic to the store.
- **SEO and PPC**: Improving search engine optimization (SEO) to rank higher in search results and using pay-per-click (PPC) ads to attract potential customers.

Seasonal Promotions

Seasonal promotions capitalize on holidays and special occasions to boost sales. Examples include:

- **Holiday Sales**: Discounts and special offers during major holidays like Diwali, Christmas, and New Year's.

- **Back-to-School Campaigns**: Promotions targeting students and parents at the start of the school year.
- **Clearance Sales**: End-of-season sales to clear out old inventory and make room for new merchandise.

5. Visual Merchandising

Visual merchandising enhances the in-store experience and attracts customers through appealing displays. Key elements include:

- **Window Displays**: Eye-catching setups in store windows to draw in passersby.
- **Product Placement**: Strategically placing products at eye level or in high-traffic areas increase visibility and sales.
- **Thematic Displays**: Creating themed displays around holidays, seasons, or special events enhance the shopping experience.

6. Events and Workshops

Events and workshops create engaging experiences that attract customers and foster community involvement. Examples include:

- **In-Store Events**: Hosting special events like product launches, celebrity appearances, or live demonstrations.
- **Workshops and Classes**: Offering educational sessions, such as cooking classes, DIY workshops, or fitness sessions, related to the store's products.

7. Cross-Promotions

Cross-promotions involve partnering with other businesses to reach a broader audience. Strategies include:

- **Collaborative Marketing**: Teaming up with local businesses to offer joint promotions discounts.
- **Co-Branding**: Partnering with well-known brands to create limited-edition products exclusive offers.

E-commerce Promotion Strategy

An effective e-commerce promotion strategy is essential for driving traffic to your online store, converting visitors into customers, and retaining them for repeat business. Here are key components to consider when developing your e-commerce promotion strategy:

Search Engine Optimization (SEO)

SEO involves optimizing your website to rank higher in search engine results. This increases organic traffic and visibility. Key tactics include:

- **Keyword Research**: Identify and use relevant keywords that potential customers are searching for.
- **On-Page Optimization**: Optimize meta titles, descriptions, headers, and content to include target keywords.
- **Technical SEO**: Ensure your site has a fast-loading speed, mobile-friendly design, and proper indexing.
- **Content Creation**: Regularly publish high-quality content such as blog posts, guides, and product descriptions.

Pay-Per-Click Advertising (PPC)

PPC advertising allows you to place ads on search engines and other platforms, paying only when someone clicks on your ad. Key strategies include:

- **Google Ads**: Use Google Ads to target specific keywords and demographics.
- **Social Media Ads**: Run targeted ads on platforms like Facebook, Instagram, and LinkedIn.
- **Retargeting**: Show ads to users who have previously visited your site to encourage them to return and make a purchase.

Social Media Marketing

Social media marketing involves using social platforms to promote your products, engage with customers, and build a community. Key tactics include:

- **Content Sharing**: Share engaging content such as posts, stories, and videos showcasing your products.
- **Influencer Collaborations**: Partner with influencers to reach a wider audience and build credibility.
- **Social Commerce**: Enable direct shopping on social media platforms through shoppable posts and ads.

- **Community Engagement**: Interact with your followers through comments, messages, and live sessions.

4. Email Marketing

Email marketing is a powerful tool for nurturing relationships with customers and driving sales. Key strategies include:

- **Segmentation**: Segment your email list based on customer behaviour, preferences, and purchase history.
- **Personalization**: Send personalized emails with tailored content and offers.
- **Automation**: Set up automated email campaigns for welcome sequences, abandoned cart reminders, and post-purchase follow-ups.
- **Exclusive Offers**: Provide special promotions and discounts to your email subscribers.

5. Content Marketing

Content marketing focuses on creating and distributing valuable content to attract and retain customers. Key tactics include:

- **Blogging**: Publish informative and engaging blog posts related to your products and industry.
- **Videos**: Create product demos, tutorials, and customer testimonials.
- **Guides and E-books**: Offer downloadable content that provides in-depth information and adds value to your customers.
- **Social Proof**: Share customer reviews, ratings, and success stories.

6. Affiliate Marketing

Affiliate marketing involves partnering with affiliates who promote your products in exchange for commission on sales. Key strategies include:

- **Affiliate Networks**: Join affiliate networks to connect with potential affiliates.
- **Commission Structure**: Set attractive commission rates to incentivize affiliates.
- **Tracking and Reporting**: Use tracking tools to monitor affiliate performance and sales.
- **Support and Resources**: Provide affiliates with marketing materials, product information and support.

Influencer Marketing

Influencer marketing leverages influencers' reach and credibility to promote your products. Key tactics include:

- **Identify Influencers**: Find influencers whose audience aligns with your target market.
- **Collaboration**: Partner with influencers for sponsored posts, product reviews, and giveaways.
- **Authenticity**: Ensure that influencer endorsements appear genuine and resonate with their followers.

Importance of Promotional Strategy

A promotional strategy is a vital component of any marketing plan. It involves the planning and execution of various marketing techniques to communicate the value of a product or service to the target audience. Here are key reasons why a promotional strategy is important:

1. **Brand Awareness**: A well-crafted promotional strategy helps increase awareness of your brand among potential customers. It ensures that your target audience knows about your product or service and recognizes your brand name, logo, and messaging.

2. **Customer Engagement**: Promotions can engage customers by providing them with compelling reasons to interact with your brand. This engagement can lead to stronger relationships and increased customer loyalty.

3. **Sales Boost**: Promotions often lead to a direct increase in sales. Limited time offers, discounts, and special deals can encourage customers to make purchases they might otherwise delay.

4. **Market Penetration**: An effective promotional strategy can help penetrate new markets by introducing your product or service to a wider audience. This is particularly important for new businesses or when launching new products.

5. **Competitive Advantage**: A well-executed promotional strategy can set your brand apart from competitors. By highlighting unique features and benefits, you can position your product as the preferred choice.

6. **Customer Retention**: Ongoing promotions and loyalty programs can keep existing customers engaged and incentivize repeat purchases, reducing customer churn.

7. **Communication of Value**: Promotions are a way to communicate the value and benefits of your product or service to the target audience. This helps in building perceived value and justifying pricing.

8. **Feedback and Improvement**: Promotions often provide opportunities for gathering customer feedback, which can be used to improve products, services, and overall customer experience.

Benefits of Promotional Strategies

Implementing effective promotional strategies offers numerous benefits for businesses. Here are some key advantages:

1. **Increased Revenue**: Promotional strategies, such as discounts and limited time offers, can lead to an immediate increase in sales and revenue. By attracting more customers and encouraging repeat purchases, businesses can boost their profitability.

2. **Customer Acquisition**: Promotions are an effective way to attract new customers. Special deals, introductory offers, and free trials can entice potential customers to try your product service for the first time.

3. **Brand Loyalty**: Loyalty programs and exclusive promotions for existing customers can foster brand loyalty. Customers who feel valued and rewarded are more likely to continue doing business with you.

4. **Market Expansion**: Promotions can help businesses expand into new markets or regions. By raising awareness and generating interest, promotions can attract customers in areas where the brand is less known.

5. **Inventory Management**: Sales promotions can help manage inventory levels by moving excess or seasonal stock. This reduces storage costs and minimizes the risk of obsolescence.

6. **Improved Customer Relationships**: Regular promotions and engagement initiatives can strengthen relationships with customers. By keeping customers engaged and interested, businesses can build a loyal customer base.

7. **Competitive Positioning**: A strong promotional strategy can differentiate your brand from competitors. Highlighting unique selling points and benefits can make your product stand out in a crowded market.

8. **Data Collection and Insights**: Promotions provide opportunities to collect valuable customer data and insights. Analysing this data can help businesses understand customer preferences, behaviours, and trends, leading to more informed marketing decisions.

9. **Enhanced Brand Image**: Effective promotions can enhance the brand image by showcasing the brand's value, innovation, and commitment to customer satisfaction. Positive experiences during promotions can lead to favourable word-of-mouth and brand reputation.

10. **Customer Engagement**: Promotional strategies that encourage customer interaction, such as contests, social media campaigns, and interactive content, can enhance customer engagement. Engaged customers are more likely to become advocates for the brand.

Unit IV: Consumer Durables

Consumer Durable Market within India

The consumer durable market in India is experiencing significant growth, driven by rising disposable incomes, urbanization, and changing lifestyles. Here are some key insights:

Market Overview

- **Growth:** The consumer durables market in India is one of the fastest-growing segments, with a projected compound annual growth rate (CAGR) of 11%. It is expected to reach Rs. 3 lakh crore (approximately $36 billion) by FY29.

- **Categories:** The market includes home appliances (like refrigerators, washing machines, and microwave ovens) and consumer electronics (like televisions, personal computers, and mobile phones).

- **Penetration:** Despite the growth, penetration levels for many appliances remain low compared to global standards. For example, only 10% of Indian households owned air conditioners as of FY24, compared to 68% in China.

Key Drivers

- **Rising Incomes:** Increased disposable incomes, especially in rural areas, are driving demand for consumer durables.
- **Urbanization:** Rapid urbanization is leading to higher consumption of durable goods.
- **Changing Lifestyles:** The shift towards nuclear families and dual-income households is increasing the need for convenience and time-saving appliances.
- **Technological Advancements:** Innovations in technology are making advanced and feature-rich products more accessible and appealing to consumers.

Challenges

- **High GST Rates:** High Goods and Services Tax (GST) rates on certain appliances, like air conditioners, classify them as luxury items, which can hinder growth.
- **Energy Efficiency:** There is a growing emphasis on energy-efficient products, with mandatory BEE star labelling for fans and other appliances.

Opportunities

- **Market Expansion:** There is significant potential for market expansion, especially in small towns and rural areas.
- **Product Innovation:** Continuous innovation in product features and sustainability can attract more consumers.
- **Government Initiatives:** Programs like the Production Linked Incentive (PLI) scheme for white goods are encouraging investment and manufacturing in the sector.

Future Outlook

- **Smart Appliances:** The demand for smart and connected appliances is expected to rise, driven by the increasing adoption of IoT and smart home technologies.
- **Export Potential:** India aims to achieve electronics manufacturing worth $300 billion and electronics exports of $120 billion by FY26.

The consumer durable market in India is poised for substantial growth, with opportunities for both domestic and international players to capitalize on the evolving consumer preferences and technological advancements.

Classification of Consumer Durables

Consumer durables, also known as durable goods, are items that have a long lifespan and are typically used over an extended period. They are broadly classified into three categories: White Goods, Brown Goods, and Shiny Goods.

1. White Goods

White Goods refer to large household appliances that are primarily used for domestic purposes. These goods are often finished in white enamel, which is how they got their name. Key examples include:

- **Refrigerators:** Used for preserving food by keeping it cool.
- **Washing Machines:** Used for laundering clothes.
- **Dishwashers:** Used for cleaning dishes and utensils.
- **Microwave Ovens:** Used for cooking and heating food.
- **Air Conditioners:** Used for cooling and maintaining indoor air quality.
- **Freezers:** Used for storing frozen food items.
- **Water Heaters:** Used for heating water.

Brown Goods

Brown Goods are electronic appliances that are used for entertainment and communication purposes. They are typically smaller than white goods and often have a brown or dark finish. Key examples include:

- **Televisions**: Used for viewing video content.
- **Audio Systems**: Used for playing music and audio.
- **DVD/Blu-ray Players**: Used for playing video discs.
- **Home Theatres**: Used for creating an immersive audiovisual experience.
- **Gaming Consoles**: Used for playing video games.
- **Computers and Laptops**: Used for a wide range of computing tasks.
- **Smartphones and Tablets**: Used for communication, entertainment, and various applications.

Shiny Goods

Shiny Goods, also known as personal care appliances or grooming products, are items that enhance personal care and grooming. These products often have a sleek and shiny finish. Key examples include:

- **Hair Dryers**: Used for drying and styling hair.
- **Electric Shavers**: Used for shaving facial and body hair.
- **Hair Straighteners**: Used for straightening hair.
- **Curling Irons**: Used for curling hair.
- **Electric Toothbrushes**: Used for dental hygiene.
- **Epilators**: Used for hair removal.
- **Personal Weighing Scales**: Used for measuring body weight.

Imports and Exports in Consumer Durable Markets

The consumer durable market in India is a dynamic sector with significant imports and exports. Here's an overview:

Imports

India imports a substantial amount of consumer durables, especially electronics and appliances, to meet domestic demand. Key points include:

- **Electronics**: India imports a variety of electronic goods, including smartphones, televisions and personal computers.
- **Home Appliances**: Items like refrigerators, washing machines, and air conditioners are also imported to cater to the growing demand.
- **Investment**: The government has been encouraging domestic manufacturing through initiatives like the Production Linked Incentive (PLI) scheme, which aims to boost local production and reduce dependency on imports.

Exports

India is also a significant exporter of consumer durables, with a growing presence in international markets:

- **Smartphones**: India has become one of the largest exporters of smartphones, with exports reaching $15.6 billion in FY24.
- **Electronics**: The electronics export market is projected to reach $120 billion by FY26.
- **Global Reach**: India's consumer electronics and appliances are exported to various countries, contributing to the country's trade balance.

Key Statistics

- **Electronics Imports**: The import value of electronic products into India has been steadily increasing, reaching significant figures over the years.
- **Export Growth**: Electronics exports from India reached $8.44 billion during the April-June 2024 quarter.
- **Market Projections**: The consumer durables market in India is expected to nearly double by 2025, reaching approximately $21.18 billion.

Durable Goods vs. Non-durable Goods

The distinction between durable and nondurable goods lies in their lifespan, usage, and the frequency with which they are purchased. Let's explore these categories in detail:

Durable Goods

Durable goods are items that have a long lifespan and can be used repeatedly over time. They are typically high-value products that are purchased infrequently. Key characteristics and examples include:

- **Lifespan**: Durable goods usually last for three years or more.

- **Usage**: These goods are intended for long-term use and often require significant investment.
- **Examples**:
    - **Home Appliances**: Refrigerators, washing machines, air conditioners.
    - **Electronics**: Televisions, computers, smartphones.
    - **Furniture**: Sofas, beds, dining tables.
    - **Vehicles**: Cars, motorcycles, bicycles.

Advantages:

- Durable goods provide long-term utility and value.
- They often come with warranties and after-sales services.
- Investments in durable goods are typically planned and budgeted.

Challenges:

- High initial cost can be a barrier for some consumers.
- Maintenance and repair may be required over the product's lifespan.
- Technological obsolescence can render some durable goods outdated.

Non-durable Goods

Nondurable goods are items that are consumed quickly and need to be purchased frequently. They have a short lifespan and are often low-cost. Key characteristics and examples include:

- **Lifespan**: Nondurable goods typically last for less than three years, often much shorter.
- **Usage**: These goods are consumed or used up quickly.
- **Examples**:
    - **Food and Beverages**: Groceries, snacks, soft drinks.
    - **Personal Care Products**: Toothpaste, shampoo, soap.
    - **Household Supplies**: Cleaning products, paper towels, detergents.
    - **Clothing and Apparel**: Everyday clothing, footwear.

Advantages:

- Non-durable goods are essential for daily living and regular consumption.
- They are usually affordable and readily available.
- Frequent purchasing can provide opportunities for brand loyalty and repeat business.

Challenges:

- Short lifespan requires continuous expenditure and regular replenishment.
- Quality and price can vary widely, impacting consumer satisfaction.
- Environmental concerns related to waste and packaging.

Economic Impact

Durable Goods:

- Durable goods are significant indicators of economic health. High demand for durable goods often signals consumer confidence and a strong economy.
- Purchases of durable goods contribute to long-term economic growth and development.
- The production of durable goods supports various industries, including manufacturing, retail and services.

Non-durable Goods:

- Non-durable goods play a crucial role in maintaining daily economic activity and consumer spending.
- The demand for nondurable goods is relatively stable and less susceptible to economic fluctuations.
- The production and distribution of nondurable goods provide consistent employment opportunities across multiple sectors.

Top Durable Goods Companies

1. Samsung

- **Products**: Electronics, home appliances, smartphones, TVs.

- **Market Presence**: Global leader in consumer electronics and home appliances.

Whirlpool

- **Products**: Washing machines, refrigerators, air conditioners.
- **Market Presence**: Major player in home appliances with a strong global footprint.

LG Electronics

- **Products**: Televisions, home appliances, mobile phones.
- **Market Presence**: Known for innovation and quality in electronics and home appliances.

Bajaj Electricals

- **Products**: Fans, lighting, kitchen appliances.
- **Market Presence**: Leading Indian company in electrical and consumer durable goods.

Voltas

- **Products**: Air conditioners, refrigerators, water coolers.
- **Market Presence**: Strong presence in the Indian market with a focus on home appliances.

Blue Star

- **Products**: Air conditioners, commercial refrigeration, water coolers.
- **Market Presence**: Renowned for its air conditioning solutions and commercial refrigeration.

Dixon Technologies

- **Products**: LED TVs, washing machines, kitchen appliances.
- **Market Presence**: Growing presence in the Indian market with a focus on manufacturing and exports.

Crompton Greaves

- **Products**: Fans, lighting, home appliances.

- **Market Presence**: Established player in the Indian consumer durable market.

9. Havells India
- **Products**: Electrical switches, fans, home appliances.
- **Market Presence**: Leading company in the Indian electrical and consumer durable sector.

10. Amber Enterprises
- **Products**: Air conditioners, refrigerators, washing machines.
- **Market Presence**: Significant player in the Indian market with a focus on manufacturing and exports.

These companies are key players in the consumer durable market, offering a wide range of products that cater to various household needs.

Credit Facility link with Consumer Durable

Credit facilities play a crucial role in the consumer durable market by making it easier for consumers to purchase high-value items. Here are some key points about how credit facilities are linked with consumer durables:

Types of Credit Facilities

1. **Consumer Durable Loans**: These are loans specifically designed to finance the purchase of consumer durables like electronics, home appliances, and furniture. They often come with features like **zero down payment, flexible repayment options**, and **minimal documentation**.

2. **EMI (Equated Monthly Instalment) Options**: Many banks and financial institutions offer EMI options on credit cards and loans, allowing consumers to pay for durable goods in instalments. This makes expensive items more affordable by spreading the cost over a period of time2.

3. **No-Cost EMI**: Some credit facilities offer no-cost EMI options, where the interest is waived off, and the consumer only pays the principal amount. This is often available for purchases above a certain amount and for a limited period.

Benefits of Credit Facilities

- **Affordability**: Credit facilities make it easier for consumers to afford high-value items by breaking down the cost into manageable monthly payments.

- **Convenience**: Consumers can purchase durable goods immediately and pay for them over time, without having to save up the full amount upfront.
- **Flexibility**: Various repayment options and tenures are available, allowing consumers to choose a plan that best suits their financial situation.
- **Instant Approval**: Many credit facilities offer instant approval and quick disbursal of funds, making the purchasing process seamless.

Popular Providers

- **HDFC Bank**: Offers Easy EMI on consumer durables, with flexible repayment options and instant approval.
- **TVS Credit**: Provides consumer durable loans with features like zero down payment and minimal documentation.
- **Paisabazaar**: Offers a range of consumer durable loans with competitive interest rates and easy application processes.

Top Consumer Durable Companies

1. **Samsung**: Known for its wide range of electronics and home appliances, including smartphones, TVs, refrigerators, and washing machines.
2. **Whirlpool**: Specializes in home appliances like washing machines, refrigerators, and air conditioners.
3. **LG Electronics**: Offers a variety of electronics and home appliances, including TVs, washing machines, and mobile phones.
4. **Bajaj Electricals**: Produces electrical appliances like fans, lighting, and kitchen appliances.
5. **Voltas**: Focuses on air conditioners, refrigerators, and water coolers.
6. **Blue Star**: Renowned for its air conditioning solutions and commercial refrigeration.
7. **Dixon Technologies**: Manufactures LED TVs, washing machines, and kitchen appliances.
8. **Crompton Greaves**: Known for fans, lighting, and home appliances.
9. **Havells India**: Offers electrical switches, fans, and home appliances.
10. **Amber Enterprises**: Specializes in air conditioners, refrigerators, and washing machines.

These companies play a significant role in the consumer durable market, providing a wide range of products that cater to various household needs.

Unit V: Consumer Personality

Definition

Consumer personality refers to the distinct psychological characteristics and traits that influence an individual's buying behaviours and preferences. It encompasses various aspects such as emotions, attitudes, and behavioural patterns that shape how consumers interact with brands, products, and services.

Understanding consumer personality helps marketers tailor their strategies to resonate with different consumer segments, enhancing engagement and loyalty. By leveraging insights into personality traits, businesses can create more personalized and effective marketing campaigns.

Personality Science in Marketing

Personality science in marketing involves understanding and leveraging psychological traits and patterns to create more effective and personalized marketing strategies. By analysing how different personality traits influence consumer behaviour, marketers can tailor their messages to resonate more deeply with their target audience1.

Key Concepts

1. **Personality Traits**: These are enduring characteristics that influence how people think, feel and behave. Common models used in marketing include the **Big Five Personality Traits** (Openness, Conscientiousness, Extraversion, Agreeableness, Neuroticism) and the **DISC Model** (Dominance, Influence, Steadiness, Conscientiousness).

2. **Behavioural Patterns**: Understanding how personality traits translate into consumer behaviours, such as purchasing decisions, brand loyalty, and product preferences.

3. **Personalized Marketing**: Using insights from personality science to create targeted marketing campaigns that speak directly to the psychological profiles of different consumer segments.

Benefits

- **Enhanced Engagement**: Personalized messages are more likely to capture attention and resonate with consumers.

- **Improved Conversion Rates**: Tailored marketing can lead to higher conversion rates as it addresses the specific needs and preferences of consumers.

- **Stronger Customer Relationships**: By understanding and catering to individual personalities, brands can build stronger, more loyal relationships with their customers.

Applications

- **Content Creation**: Crafting content that aligns with the personality traits of the target audience.
- **Product Recommendations**: Offering personalized product suggestions based on consumer personality profiles.
- **Customer Segmentation**: Dividing the market into segments based on personality traits to create more focused marketing strategies.

Ethical Considerations

- **Privacy**: Ensuring that data collection and usage comply with privacy laws and ethical standards.
- **Transparency**: Being transparent with consumers about how their data is being used and for what purposes.

By integrating personality science into marketing strategies, businesses can create more meaningful and impactful connections with their audience, ultimately driving better business outcomes.

Buyer Persona to Optimize Customer Journey

A **buyer persona** is a semi-fictional representation of your ideal customer based on market research and real data about your existing customers. Developing detailed buyer personas helps businesses understand their customers better and tailor their marketing strategies to meet their needs effectively. When used to optimize the customer journey, buyer personas can greatly enhance customer satisfaction and conversion rates. Here's how:

Understanding Customer Needs and Preferences

By creating buyer personas, businesses can gain insights into their customers' needs, preferences, pain points, and behaviours. This understanding allows for more precise targeting and personalized communication throughout the customer journey.

Tailoring Marketing Messages

Buyer personas enable marketers to craft messages that resonate with specific segments of th audience. Personalized messages that address the unique needs and motivations of different person are more likely to engage and convert.

3. Enhancing Customer Experience

With buyer personas, businesses can map out the customer journey more effectively. They can ident key touchpoints and interactions that matter most to their personas and optimize these touchpoi to provide a seamless and satisfying experience.

4. Creating Relevant Content

Content marketing efforts can be tailored to match the interests and preferences of different buy personas. By providing relevant and valuable content at each stage of the customer journey, business can nurture leads and guide them towards a purchase decision.

5. Improving Product Development

Understanding the specific needs and challenges of different buyer personas can inform produ development. Businesses can design and develop products that better meet the expectations a requirements of their target audience.

Steps to Create and Use Buyer Personas

1. **Research and Data Collection**
   - Gather information about your customers through surveys, interviews, and analytic
   - Identify common characteristics, behaviours, and preferences.

2. **Identify Key Personas**
   - Segment your audience based on the data collected.
   - Create detailed profiles for each key persona, including demographics, goa challenges, and preferred communication channels.

3. **Map the Customer Journey**

- Identify the stages of the customer journey for each persona, from awareness to purchase and beyond.
- Pinpoint key touchpoints and interactions at each stage.

4. **Tailor Marketing Strategies**
    - Develop marketing messages and content that align with the needs and preferences of each persona.
    - Use personalized communication to engage with personas at different stages of the journey.

5. **Optimize Touchpoints**
    - Ensure that each touchpoint along the customer journey is optimized to provide a positive experience.
    - Address any pain points and enhance the overall customer journey.

6. **Monitor and Adjust**
    - Continuously gather feedback and data to refine and update your buyer personas.
    - Adjust your marketing strategies and customer journey mapping based on new insights.

Brand Personality

Brand personality refers to the set of human characteristics and traits that a brand embodies and communicates to its audience. Just like individuals, brands can have personalities that influence how they are perceived by consumers. A strong and well-defined brand personality helps to create an emotional connection with the target audience, differentiate the brand from competitors, and foster brand loyalty. Here are the key components and benefits of brand personality:

Key Components

1. **Characteristics and Traits**: Brands can possess various characteristics that are typically associated with human personalities. These may include traits such as trustworthiness, sophistication, excitement, ruggedness, and sincerity. These traits help consumers relate to the brand on a personal level.

2. **Consistency**: A consistent brand personality across all touchpoints – from marketing communications to customer service – reinforces the brand's identity and builds trust with consumers. Consistency ensures that the brand personality remains recognizable and reliable.

3. **Emotional Appeal**: Brand personality creates an emotional appeal by resonating with the values, lifestyles, and aspirations of the target audience. This emotional connection can lead to stronger brand loyalty and advocacy.

4. **Differentiation**: A unique brand personality differentiates the brand from competitors. It helps the brand stand out in a crowded market and creates a distinct identity that consumers can identify with.

Benefits

1. **Brand Loyalty**: Consumers are more likely to develop a strong bond with brands that have relatable and appealing personalities. This bond leads to increased brand loyalty and repeat purchases.

2. **Higher Engagement**: Brands with well-defined personalities tend to engage consumers more effectively. Whether through social media interactions, advertising, or customer experience, a strong brand personality can capture and maintain consumer attention.

3. **Word-of-Mouth**: A compelling brand personality can encourage positive word-of-mouth recommendations. Satisfied customers are more likely to share their experiences with friends and family, further promoting the brand.

4. **Price Premium**: Consumers are often willing to pay a premium for brands that have strong and appealing personalities. The perceived value of the brand increases, allowing for higher pricing without losing customers.

Examples of Brand Personalities

1. **Apple**: Apple's brand personality is characterized by innovation, sophistication, and creativity. The brand is seen as cutting-edge and premium, appealing to consumers who value technology and design.

2. **Nike**: Nike's personality embodies athleticism, motivation, and inspiration. The brand encourages consumers to "Just Do It," appealing to those who are passionate about sports and fitness.

3. **Coca-Cola**: Coca-Cola's brand personality is cheerful, friendly, and inclusive. The brand promotes happiness and enjoyment, making it relatable to a wide audience.

4. **Harley-Davidson**: Harley-Davidson's personality is rugged, adventurous, and rebellious. The brand appeals to consumers who identify with freedom and the open road.

Extroversion and Impulsive Buying

Extroversion is a personality trait characterized by sociability, talkativeness, assertiveness, and high levels of emotional expressiveness. Individuals who score high on extroversion are often energetic, enthusiastic, and enjoy being around others. This trait significantly influences consumer behaviour, particularly in the context of impulsive buying.

Key Characteristics of Extroverts in Consumer Behaviour

1. **Sociability**: Extroverts tend to seek social interactions and enjoy shopping as a social activity. They are more likely to shop with friends and family, making the shopping experience enjoyable and exciting.
2. **Impulsiveness**: Extroverts are often more spontaneous and prone to make quick decisions without extensive deliberation. This impulsiveness can lead to unplanned purchases, especially when they encounter attractive deals or promotions.
3. **Emotional Expressiveness**: Extroverts are expressive and tend to respond to emotional stimuli. They are more likely to be influenced by advertisements that evoke positive emotions and excitement.
4. **Stimulation Seeking**: Extroverts enjoy variety and new experiences. They are drawn to new products, innovations, and unique shopping experiences, making them more likely to make impulsive purchases when something novel catches their eye.

Impulsive Buying and Extroversion

Impulsive buying refers to spontaneous, unplanned purchases driven by immediate desires rather than pre-existing intentions. Extroverts are particularly susceptible to impulsive buying for several reasons:

1. **Social Influence**: Extroverts are more likely to be influenced by social interactions and peer pressure. When shopping with friends, they may make impulsive purchases to align with the group or gain social approval.
2. **Positive Emotions**: Extroverts often seek positive emotional experiences. Retail environments that create excitement and positive feelings can trigger impulsive buying behaviour in extroverts.
3. **Advertising Impact**: Extroverts are more responsive to advertisements that use emotional appeal, excitement, and vibrant visuals. Effective advertising can create a sense of urgency and excitement, leading to impulsive purchases.
4. **Low Self-Control**: While not exclusive to extroverts, lower self-control is associated with impulsive buying. Extroverts, due to their spontaneous nature, may exhibit lower self-control in shopping scenarios, leading to unplanned purchases.

Marketing Strategies for Extroverts

To appeal to extroverts and potentially increase impulsive buying, marketers can employ several strategies:

1. **Create Engaging Experiences**: Design retail environments and online shopping platforms that are vibrant, interactive, and socially engaging. In-store events, product launches, and social media campaigns can attract extroverts.

2. **Emotional Advertising**: Use advertisements that evoke strong positive emotions, excitement, and enjoyment. Highlighting social aspects and experiences in ads can resonate well with extroverts.

3. **Limited-Time Offers**: Implement promotions that create a sense of urgency, such as flash sales, limited-time discounts, and exclusive deals. These can trigger impulsive buying by appealing to extroverts' desire for immediate gratification.

4. **Social Proof**: Showcase customer reviews, testimonials, and user-generated content. Seeing others enjoying the product or service can influence extroverts' purchasing decisions and encourage impulsive buying.

Agreeableness and Word-of-Mouth Influence

Agreeableness is a personality trait characterized by warmth, kindness, empathy, and a tendency to get along well with others. Individuals high in agreeableness are often cooperative, friendly, and value social harmony. This trait significantly influences consumer behaviour, especially in the context of word-of-mouth (WOM) communication and recommendations.

Key Characteristics of Agreeable Consumers

1. **Empathy**: Agreeable individuals are empathetic and considerate of others' feelings. This makes them more likely to share positive experiences and recommend products that they believe can benefit others.

2. **Trustworthiness**: People with high agreeableness are seen as trustworthy and reliable by others. Their recommendations are often valued and taken seriously by their social circles.

3. **Altruism**: Agreeable consumers have a natural inclination to help others. They often engage in word-of-mouth marketing out of a genuine desire to assist friends and family in making good purchasing decisions.

4. **Cooperation**: Agreeable individuals prefer cooperative and collaborative interactions. They are more likely to participate in social activities and discussions, including sharing their opinions about products and services.

Word-of-Mouth Influence

Word-of-mouth influence refers to the impact of personal recommendations and conversations on consumer behaviour. It is one of the most powerful forms of marketing, as people tend to trust the opinions of friends, family, and peers more than traditional advertising.

1. **Positive WOM**: Agreeable consumers are more likely to spread positive word-of-mouth. They share their positive experiences and recommend products they find valuable, contributing to brand awareness and trust.
2. **Customer Loyalty**: Positive word-of-mouth from agreeable individuals can lead to increased customer loyalty. When consumers hear about the positive experiences of others, they are more likely to trust the brand and become loyal customers.
3. **Social Proof**: Recommendations from agreeable consumers serve as social proof. Potential buyers are influenced by the positive feedback and are more likely to try the product themselves.
4. **Online Reviews and Ratings**: Agreeable individuals are also more likely to leave positive reviews and high ratings online. These reviews can significantly influence the purchasing decisions of other consumers who rely on online feedback.

Marketing Strategies to Leverage Agreeableness

1. **Encourage Reviews and Testimonials**: Encourage agreeable customers to share their positive experiences through reviews and testimonials. Provide incentives, such as discounts or loyalty points, to motivate them.
2. **Create Referral Programs**: Develop referral programs that reward customers for recommending your products to others. This can leverage the natural altruism and cooperative nature of agreeable consumers.
3. **Highlight Social Impact**: Emphasize the social and community benefits of your products. Agreeable consumers are more likely to support brands that contribute positively to society and promote social harmony.
4. **Foster Community Engagement**: Build and nurture a community around your brand. Use social media platforms, forums, and events to create spaces where agreeable individuals can share their experiences and recommendations.
5. **Personalized Thank-You Notes**: Sending personalized thank-you notes or appreciation messages to customers who leave positive reviews can reinforce their behaviour and encourage future word-of-mouth promotion.

Conscientiousness and Brand Loyalty

Conscientiousness is one of the five major personality traits in the Big Five Personality Trait model. It is characterized by high levels of thoughtfulness, good impulse control, goal-directed behaviours, and a preference for planned rather than spontaneous activities. Individuals who score high on conscientiousness are often organized, reliable, and dependable. This personality trait has significant impact on consumer behaviour, particularly in the context of brand loyalty.

Key Characteristics of Conscientious Consumers

1. **Reliability:** Conscientious individuals value reliability and consistency. They prefer brands that consistently deliver high-quality products and services.
2. **Trustworthiness**: These consumers are likely to remain loyal to brands they trust and have had positive experiences with.
3. **Goal-Oriented**: Conscientious consumers are goal-oriented and make purchasing decisions based on long-term benefits rather than impulsive desires.
4. **Attention to Detail:** They pay close attention to details, such as product features, reviews and brand reputation, before making a purchase decision.
5. **Planning and Organization**: Conscientious consumers prefer well-planned purchases and often engage in thorough research before committing to a brand.

Impact on Brand Loyalty

Brand loyalty refers to a consumer's commitment to repurchase or continue using a particular brand. Conscientious consumers tend to exhibit strong brand loyalty due to several factors:

1. **Consistency in Quality**: Brands that consistently deliver high-quality products and services are more likely to retain conscientious consumers. These individuals appreciate consistency and reliability, leading to repeat purchases.
2. **Positive Experiences**: Conscientious consumers value positive interactions with brands. Excellent customer service, seamless shopping experiences, and dependable after-sales support contribute to building loyalty.
3. **Long-Term Relationships**: Conscientious consumers are more likely to develop long-term relationships with brands they trust. They prioritize established brands that have a proven track record of meeting their expectations.
4. **Detailed Research**: Before committing to a brand, conscientious consumers conduct thorough research. Brands that provide comprehensive product information, transparent practices, and positive reviews are more likely to earn their loyalty.

5. **Emphasis on Values**: Conscientious individuals often align themselves with brands that reflect their personal values and ethical standards. Brands that demonstrate social responsibility and ethical practices can build strong loyalty among these consumers.

Strategies to Foster Brand Loyalty Among Conscientious Consumers

1. **Maintain Consistency**: Ensure that your brand consistently delivers high-quality products and services. Conscientious consumers appreciate reliability and are likely to stay loyal to brands they can depend on.
2. **Focus on Customer Service**: Provide exceptional customer service and support. Positive interactions with the brand can reinforce loyalty and trust.
3. **Transparency and Honesty**: Be transparent about your products, practices, and policies. Conscientious consumers value honesty and are more likely to trust brands that are open and transparent.
4. **Provide Detailed Information**: Offer comprehensive product information, including features, benefits, and usage guidelines. Detailed descriptions and specifications help conscientious consumers make informed decisions.
5. **Highlight Ethical Practices**: Emphasize your brand's commitment to ethical practices, sustainability, and social responsibility. Conscientious consumers are more likely to support brands that align with their values.
6. **Encourage Feedback**: Actively seek and act on customer feedback. Demonstrating that you value and respond to customer input can enhance loyalty among conscientious consumers.
7. **Reward Loyalty**: Implement loyalty programs that reward repeat customers. Providing incentives for continued patronage can reinforce brand loyalty.

Interrelated Behaviour

Interrelated behaviour in consumer personality refers to the complex interplay between different personality traits and how they influence purchasing decisions and consumption patterns. Understanding these interrelations can help marketers develop more nuanced and effective strategies. Here are some key aspects:

Key Personality Traits and Their Interactions

1. **Extraversion and Agreeableness**
    - **Extraversion**: Sociable, energetic, and outgoing individuals.
    - **Agreeableness**: Cooperative, friendly, and empathetic individuals.

- **Interrelation**: Extraverted and agreeable individuals are more likely to engage in soc[ial] shopping experiences, seek recommendations, and provide positive word-of-mou[th]. They enjoy group activities and are influenced by social proof.

2. **Conscientiousness and Neuroticism**
   - **Conscientiousness**: Organized, reliable, and goal-oriented individuals.
   - **Neuroticism**: Anxious, emotional, and easily stressed individuals.
   - **Interrelation**: Conscientious consumers are thorough in their research and planni[ng] while neurotic consumers may exhibit cautious purchasing behaviour. Combin[ing] these traits can result in careful decision-making, seeking reassurance through revie[ws] and brand reputation.

3. **Openness and Conscientiousness**
   - **Openness**: Creative, open to new experiences, and curious individuals.
   - **Conscientiousness**: Detail-oriented and disciplined individuals.
   - **Interrelation**: Consumers high in both traits are adventurous yet systematic. They a[re] open to trying new products but do so with careful consideration and planning. Th[ey] value innovative products that also offer practical benefits.

4. **Agreeableness and Neuroticism**
   - **Agreeableness**: Cooperative and empathetic.
   - **Neuroticism**: Emotional and anxious.
   - **Interrelation**: Agreeable and neurotic individuals may seek brands that provide [a] sense of comfort and reassurance. They are likely to be loyal to brands that off[er] consistent quality and positive customer experiences.

Implications for Marketing

Understanding the interplay between different personality traits can help marketers tailor the[ir] strategies more effectively:

1. **Personalized Marketing**: Develop personalized campaigns that resonate with the speci[fic] combination of traits exhibited by target consumers. For example, content that appeals to bo[th] the adventurous nature of open individuals and the detailed orientation of conscientio[us] consumers.

2. **Product Positioning**: Position products in a way that highlights their appeal to multiple trai[ts]. For instance, innovative features for open consumers and reliability for conscientious ones.

3. **Customer Segmentation**: Segment customers based on combinations of traits to create more accurate and effective marketing strategies.
4. **Communication Strategies**: Use communication that addresses the emotional needs of neurotic consumers while emphasizing the cooperative and supportive aspects appreciated by agreeable consumers.
5. **Experience Design**: Design shopping experiences that cater to social and emotional needs. For example, create engaging, social shopping environments for extraverted and agreeable consumers.

Cognitive Patterns in Consumer Personality

Cognitive patterns refer to the mental processes and structures that influence how individuals perceive, think, and make decisions. Understanding these cognitive patterns in consumer personality helps marketers create strategies that align with how consumers process information and make purchasing decisions.

Here are some key cognitive patterns in consumer personality:

Perception

Perception is the process by which consumers select, organize, and interpret information. It influences how consumers view and interpret marketing messages, product attributes, and brand information. Key factors include:

- **Selective Attention**: Consumers focus on specific information while ignoring others. Effective marketing must capture and retain consumer attention.
- **Selective Distortion**: Consumers interpret information in a way that aligns with their existing beliefs and attitudes.
- **Selective Retention**: Consumers remember information that supports their beliefs and forget information that contradicts them.

Motivation

Motivation drives consumers to fulfil their needs and desires. It influences the urgency and type of products consumers are inclined to buy. Key concepts include:

- **Maslow's Hierarchy of Needs**: Consumers prioritize their needs from basic (physiological) to higher-level (self-actualization).
- **Intrinsic and Extrinsic Motivation**: Intrinsic motivation is driven by internal satisfaction, while extrinsic motivation is driven by external rewards.

3. Learning

Learning involves changes in behaviour resulting from experiences. It shapes how consumers respond to marketing stimuli based on past experiences. Key concepts include:

- **Classical Conditioning**: Associating a brand with positive stimuli to elicit a favourable response.
- **Operant Conditioning**: Using rewards and reinforcements to encourage desired behaviour.
- **Cognitive Learning**: Involves problem-solving and thinking, where consumers use information to make decisions.

4. Attitudes and Beliefs

Attitudes and beliefs are formed through experiences and influence consumer behaviour. They determine how consumers feel about products and brands. Key components include:

- **Cognitive Component**: Beliefs and knowledge about a product or brand.
- **Affective Component**: Emotional responses and feelings towards a product or brand.
- **Behavioural Component**: Intentions and actions towards a product or brand.

5. Decision-Making Process

The **decision-making process** involves several stages through which consumers go before making a purchase. These stages include:

- **Problem Recognition**: Identifying a need or problem.
- **Information Search**: Seeking information about potential solutions.
- **Evaluation of Alternatives**: Comparing different products or brands.
- **Purchase Decision**: Making the final purchase choice.
- **Post-Purchase Behaviour**: Evaluating the purchase experience and product satisfaction.

6. Heuristics and Biases

Consumers use **heuristics** (mental shortcuts) and are subject to **cognitive biases** when making decisions. Understanding these can help marketers predict and influence consumer behaviour. Key examples include:

- **Anchoring Bias**: Relying heavily on the first piece of information received.

- **Confirmation Bias**: Favouring information that confirms existing beliefs.
- **Availability Heuristic**: Basing decisions on readily available information or recent experiences.

Implications for Marketing

1. **Tailored Communication**: Develop marketing messages that align with consumers' perceptual processes, ensuring that key information is prominently featured and easy to understand.
2. **Motivational Appeals**: Craft campaigns that address consumers' intrinsic and extrinsic motivations, appealing to their core needs and desires.
3. **Learning and Reinforcement**: Use conditioning techniques to build positive associations with the brand and reinforce desired consumer behaviours.
4. **Attitude Formation**: Focus on shaping positive attitudes by providing consistent, reliable information and fostering emotional connections with the brand.
5. **Simplified Decision-Making**: Streamline the decision-making process by offering clear comparisons, highlighting benefits, and reducing complexity.
6. **Addressing Biases**: Recognize and leverage cognitive biases and heuristics to guide consumer decisions, such as using anchoring in pricing strategies or creating urgency to leverage the availability heuristic.

Classification of Consumer Personality

Consumer personality can be classified using several psychological frameworks and models that help understand individual differences in behaviour, preferences, and decision-making processes. Here are some of the most used classifications:

Big Five Personality Traits (OCEAN Model)

The **Big Five Personality Traits** model is one of the most widely accepted frameworks in psychology. It classifies personality into five broad dimensions:

1. **Openness to Experience**
    - Characteristics: Creative, curious, open to new experiences.
    - Consumer Behaviour: Likely to try new products and brands, prefers innovative and unique items.

2. **Conscientiousness**
    - Characteristics: Organized, disciplined, goal oriented.
    - Consumer Behaviour: Prefers reliable and high-quality products, makes we researched and planned purchases.

3. **Extraversion**
    - Characteristics: Sociable, outgoing, energetic.
    - Consumer Behaviour: Influenced by social interactions, enjoys shopping as a soc activity, tends to make impulsive purchases.

4. **Agreeableness**
    - Characteristics: Kind, cooperative, empathetic.
    - Consumer Behaviour: Prefers brands that are ethical and socially responsible, relies word-of-mouth recommendations.

5. **Neuroticism**
    - Characteristics: Anxious, emotional, easily stressed.
    - Consumer Behaviour: Seeks reassurance through brand trust and positive reviews, m be cautious in purchasing decisions.

2. Myers-Briggs Type Indicator (MBTI)

The **MBTI** classifies personality into 16 distinct types based on four dichotomies:

1. **Extraversion (E) vs. Introversion (I)**
    - Extraverts are outgoing and sociable, while introverts are reserved and reflective.
2. **Sensing (S) vs. Intuition (N)**
    - Sensing individuals focus on concrete information, while intuitive individuals look the big picture and abstract concepts.
3. **Thinking (T) vs. Feeling (F)**
    - Thinkers' base decisions on logic and objective criteria, while feelers prioritize person values and emotions.

4. **Judging (J) vs. Perceiving (P)**
   - Judging individuals prefer structure and organization, while perceiving individuals are more flexible and spontaneous.

Each MBTI type combination provides insights into consumer preferences and behaviours.

VALS Framework (Values and Lifestyles)

The **VALS** framework segments consumers based on their values, attitudes, and lifestyles. It identifies eight distinct consumer segments:

1. **Innovators**: High resources and high innovation; seek new products and experiences.
2. **Thinkers**: Motivated by ideals; value knowledge and order.
3. **Believers**: Motivated by ideals; value consistency and predictability.
4. **Achievers**: Motivated by success; value products that demonstrate success.
5. **Strivers**: Motivated by achievement; seek approval from others.
6. **Experiencers**: Motivated by self-expression; seek excitement and adventure.
7. **Makers**: Motivated by self-expression; value practicality and self-sufficiency.
8. **Survivors**: Low resources; focused on meeting basic needs.

DISC Model

The **DISC** model classifies personality based on four primary traits:

1. **Dominance (D)**: Assertive, results-oriented, and competitive.
   - Consumer Behaviour: Prefers efficient and performance-driven products.
2. **Influence (I)**: Sociable, enthusiastic, and persuasive.
   - Consumer Behaviour: Influenced by social proof and brand reputation.
3. **Steadiness (S)**: Patient, cooperative, and dependable.
   - Consumer Behaviour: Prefers stable and reliable brands, values loyalty.
4. **Conscientiousness (C)**: Analytical, detail-oriented, and accurate.
   - Consumer Behaviour: Makes informed and well-researched purchasing decisions.

www.ingramcontent.com/pod-product-compliance
Lightning Source LLC
Chambersburg PA
CBHW070939220526
45469CB00007B/2440